Goddess Alpha
Directions Home

Jessica Theroux

DURVILE &
UpRoute

Calgary, Alberta, Canada

DURVILE &
UpRoute

UpRoute Imprint of Durvile Publications Ltd.
Calgary, Alberta, Canada
durvile.com

Library and Archives Cataloging

Goddess Alpha: Directions Home
Theroux, Jessica; Author and Artist
Eliot, Winslow PhD; Foreword

1. Goddess | 2. Mind Body Spirit | 3. Inspiration | 4. Needlework | 5. Embroidery

The "Every River Lit" Series, Ways of Light. Series Editor, Lorene Shyba PhD

ISBN: 978-1-990735-44-8 (pbk); 978-1-990735-58-5 (e-pub); 978-1-990735-59-2 (audiobook)

The lands where our studios stand in southern Alberta are part of the ancient homeland and traditional territory of many Indigenous Nations; places of hunting, travel, trade, and healing. Treaty 7 Nations are Siksika, Piikani, and Kainai of the Niisitapi (Blackfoot) Confederacy; Dene Tsuut'ina; and Chiniki, Bearspaw, and Wesley Stoney Nakoda First Nations. We also acknowledge the homeland of the Métis Nation of Alberta. We commit to serving the needs of Indigenous Peoples today and into the future.

Durvile Publications acknowledges financial support for book development and production from the Government of Canada through Canadian Heritage, Canada Book Fund and the Government of Alberta, Alberta Media Fund.
Printed in India. First edition. First Printing.

DURVILE.COM

Dedication

This book is for you.
Goddess Alpha serves as a reminder that in this world, it is easy to forget
You have an army behind you.
These are your directions home;
breadcrumbs to always remember your way back.

Acknowledgments

My goddess research is an amalgamation of received stories, conversations, listening, speaking, reading, and writing over decades, spun together with lived and learned experience, imagination, and curiosity. Goddess Alpha is more than a historical account and collection of facts. It is an act of fantasy, and respect.

I extend special gratitude to the wonderful storytellers who have influenced me greatly: Clarissa Pinkola Estes, Jean Shinoda Bolen, Joseph Campbell and Alexander Eliot, to name a few. Thank you to Lorene Shyba for her faith and mystical vision. Thank you to my parents, Garry and Debbie Szabo, for being my origin story and place of my first learning when it came to stories and the power of myth and, of course, for your unwavering support every day, helping with photography and ironing and anything I ask of you; my solid foundation.

Thank you to Winslow Eliot and Islene Runningdeer for the uplifting and esoteric fresh eyes in this journey. Thank you to my grandmothers who showed me the power of telling stories with my hands.

Final gratitude goes to my husband, Rich Théroux, for the gift of a life well lived. You are the fire in the hearth of my home and along with all these breadcrumbs I am able to travel, and dance, and explore, and never worry about finding my way safely back.

Foreword

- - - -

Jess Theroux has compiled a contemporary text that encompasses the complexities and richness of our inner worlds as reflected in these extraordinary and ancient goddesses. A wonderful gift for coming-of-age women, it is also a book that's a powerful guide for people of all ages and genders. As the author describes Venus, it's "perfect."

Jess captures the essential qualities of these goddesses from around the world in fresh, unique, artistic, and insightful ways. Through intuitive and knowledgeable descriptions, beautiful poetry, unique artwork, and compassionate guidance, she shows us how to befriend each one. She offers us a fierce, loving insight into the goddesses and into ourselves. Her words—and accompanying symbols—feel as true as the arrows that Artemis lets fly.

Chaos reminds us to
Find comfort in the unknown
In the in between

—Winslow Eliot, PhD, metaphysician, and author of
Be Still—how to heal and grow and
What Would You Do If There Was Nothing You Had To Do

Preface

In 2017, I was teaching an art class and we were looking at font design. For an example in class, I designed an alphabet, each letter based on a goddess. As I embroidered each letter, whether at school or at our Rumble House gallery, I would tell the stories of who I was focusing on at that moment. These letters were important; representative of huge and universal truths. When I had a stack of 26 letters, little linen rectangles, I decided to make a book out of them.

It took a year to put the whole thing together, write the poems to accompany the letters, and design each page based on the various cultures. This was a practice in digging for truth and connecting to ideas, not about perfection. It was all intuition and heart. Making the book was a balance between economy—too many fabric pages to hide the backs of the embroidery would make the book too thick, versus freeing myself from expectations of the past. There are threads showing and knots to fiddle with.

For years I carried this book around with me in my backpack and purse. I would tell the stories when people asked. Tapping into rich connectivity to a central flow of feminine energy, the lessons I wanted to remember were laid out in 52 pages of string, and colour, and love.

When the ability to share this with more people came, it was intimidating and exciting. This book is an opportunity to expand on free-verse poetry and create daily routines to keep our power in the forefront of our consciousness. As you practice these reflections they will become second nature and part of who you are. Work towards a connection with everything around you. Meditate on home. Find peace and the goddess within.   —Jessica Theroux, 2024

Goddesses, A to M

Artemis .
Page 8

Bilquis
Page 12

Chaos .
Page 16

Dakini .
Page 20

Eos .
Page 24

Freya .
Page 28

Gaia .
Page 32

Hecate.
Page 36

Inanna .
Page 40

Jezabel .
Page 44

Kali.
Page 48

La Loba .
Page 52

Mary .
Page 56

Goddesses, N to Z

Na'ashjé'ii Asdzáá

Page 60

O Erdőben

Page 64

Persephone

Page 68

Qallupilluk

Page 72

Rhiannon

Page 76

Sekmet

Page 80

Tanit

Page 84

Urania

Page 88

Venus

Page 92

Wuriupranili

Page 96

Xihe

Page 100

Yamuna

Page 104

Zorya Sisters

Page 108

This book is to serve as a reminder. In this world it is easy to forget. You have an army behind you. Remember.

Artemis, she reminds us that nature is our temple, the wilderness, our holy place. Her bow & arrow reminds us to be true. Her crescent moon reminds us to be light bringers. Most importantly, she calls on us to support and protect the feminine.

I AM ARTEMIS

I am wild, one with the wilderness
A delectable balance of timing
And immaculate chaos
One with the natural cycles
My home was Ancient Greece
And now I live in the hearts of those who
    protect Mother Earth
I am Alpha Huntress
No hunter comes before me
Those animals I get to know
We agree on terms
To survive, you never take more than you need
To thrive, you take what wants to be taken
I am
    The Boar
    The Stag
    The Bear
I am the moon and all her cycles
The crescent moon is the bend of my bow
My arrow is my truth
My needle piercing the silence
Resolute and unwavering

I am the new moon
The promise of the light coming, new beginnings
I took my vow of celibacy, my partner is nature
Water over rocks is my music
I stand for truth
The wilderness holds that truth
Come to my home and you'll feel
That truth, the breeze through the windows
You'll feel safe to be you
Artemisia plants: tarragon, mugwort, wormwood,
Burning to cleanse the air, in pastes in glass jars
These plants, for fevers, inflammation, headaches
The extra bed is always made for visitors
The antlers and feathers and furs
Adorning my home are gifts from the animals
When you build your altars
Remember the ethical journey of only receiving
What is given to you in jubilance
You can't force connection, you can't fake holy
My home is a place where you can be you
When people come to me in honesty
They are received with love and compassion
Including you
I am with you.

REFLECT

What are distractions
   in your life right now?
What is hindering you from being your truest self?
Breathe deep
Who is your truest self?
What elements are strong in you?
What elements need nurturing?
Are there distractions that could be re-focused,
   and used as opportunities for re-centring?
For example: dishes could be stopping you from
   writing your novel, but could you use that time
   to listen to a podcast or a favorite album? Or
   dictate notes? A time to meditate on big ideas?

ACT

Venture into nature
Carve out time to be quiet outside
with family or alone
summer or winter
you need fresh air
grass between your toes
dirt under your fingernails
snow in your hair
Remember me, feel the pulse of the mother
Protect and lift up your sisters

MEDITATE

Wherever you are, close your eyes
Breathe deep, imagine the fresh scent of
   new growth in a deep forest
Breathe deep
imagine the soft mossy earth below you
feel the wind around you, gentle,
just enough to make the trees whisper
Remember me
The new-moon sky may be dark,
The light is coming. Be the light
You are armed with the truth
I am at your side.

Bilquis reminds us of our sexual power. While it will manifest differently for everyone, we must never be made to feel ashamed.

Protect and honour that connection between you and the Goddess.

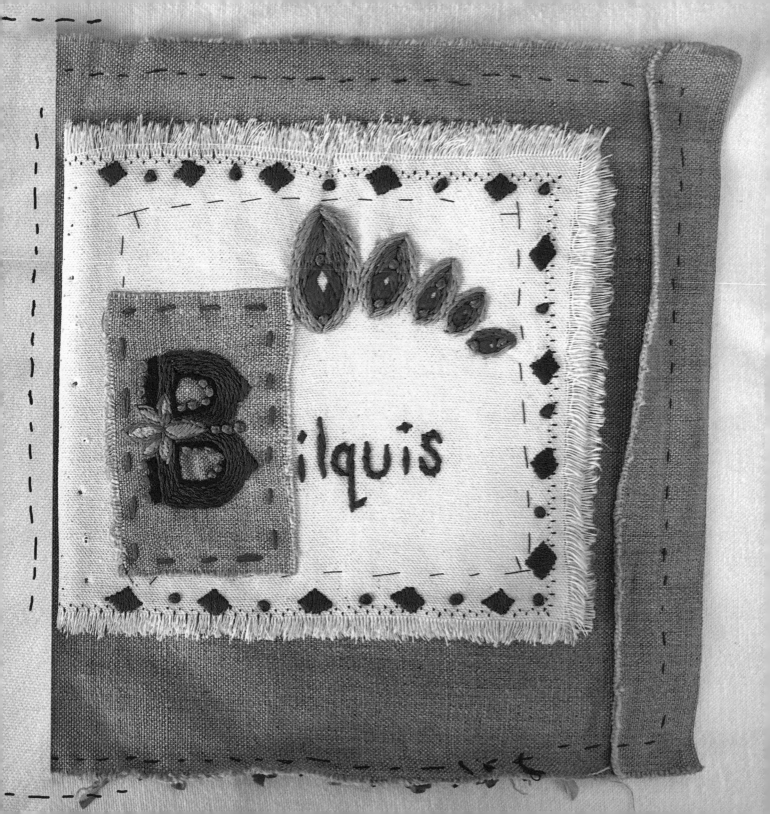

I AM BILQUIS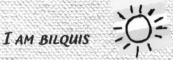

The Queen of Sheba
I am the daughter of a jinn and my mother
    was a queen.
I know political and sexual power, both.
I am known for how much I have, and yet
    I am still ravenously hungry for more,
    more knowledge, more experience
Any way to grow beyond
I come from what is now Ethiopia
I am the beginning of a long line of Kings
They wrote about me in the Hebrew Bible,
    the Qur'an and the Kebra Nagast
All different words for the same story
There was a woman
She upset the norm
She had hairy legs and beautiful hips
She was evil
Evilly intelligent
Wildly out of control
    a wealthy monarch
    a philosopher-queen
    a heretic!

There are so many stories, they called me lustful
    and indulgent.
A tapestry of histories
And intentions
I guess there was a little bit of me in each story
My home is beautiful, everything gold and shining
I would travel, and people would travel to me
I have many treasures from across the world.
I have musicians playing for me always
Sitars and zithers
I sing as I work around the home
Frankincense smoke spiraling
    through the notes of my song
I worship the sun
The only celestial body to
Rival me
And my gold
These monotheists come around
And push their god
But it's the sun that catches my eye
Do what brings you belly jiggling joy
What gives you butterflies?
Do that and I'll be with you.

REFLECT

Who are you really?
What helps you feel alive?
What excites you?
What turns you on?
Are you getting everything you desire?
If not, what's stopping you?
How can you restructure things in your life to attract
    elements you crave?
Reflect on the various stories of you that will
    surface after your death
What stories do you want people to remember?

ACT

Stretch. Reconnect with every inch of yourself.
First your body, roll out your joints, next your mind.
Listen to voices outside your usual experience
While in a safe space, push yourself to be
    uncomfortable
Do riddles
Have you been wanting to train for a marathon?
Buy running shoes.
Have you been curious about a book that seemed
    outside your comfort zone? Read it.
Have you been curious about faith?
From a place of Love and Compassion, journey to a
    new land and learn everything you can
EXPAND.

MEDITATE

No matter what time of year, find a quiet place to
    close your eyes
Breathe deep
    imagine heat, dry desert heat, slow down
    imagine the tongues of sunshine on you
    smell rich and earthy scents
    Myrrh, Sandalwood, Cinnamon
    settle in, breathe slow, slow everything down
Remember me
My insatiable thirst for knowledge, for experience,
    and understanding
You have sexual power and royalty in your blood
Back straight, head high, I am at your side

Chaos reminds us to
find comfort in the unknown,
in the in between,
in the fog.

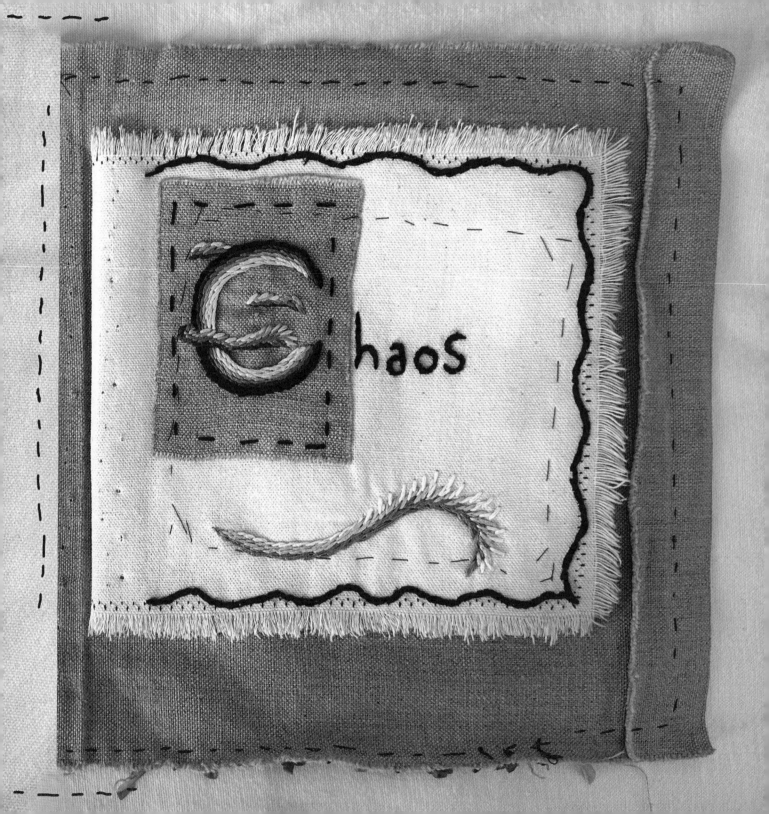

I AM CHAOS

I am Primordial
Fog and mist
Alpha
    "the chasm" between heaven and Earth
They've called me a chaotic mix of elements
Existing in the primordial universe
    primal mud
I am the fertile space from where life sprang
The misty air through which birds fly
I am the beginning
Before form
I am complex and crude and cunning
I smell like ozone
Like earth and rain like dark dreams
I speak through all the mouths
See through all the eyes
My home is before the beginning
Timeless, formless, limitless.

I existed before mouths and eyes
I speak through your cells
Do you hear me?
Whispering in languages never written down
Through the winds
Between the dust
Spinning yarn from the ether
I am reminding you of the beginning
There were no words
To misinterpret
There was only essence
And things built from there
Or they didn't
Accepting when things don't work
Understanding that when things
Do work
knowing it is the universe at play
The big bang began it all and we
Are just little bangs
Creating as we grow.

REFLECT

What contrasting
    binaries are at play in you? introvert? extrovert?
Chaos reminds you of the in between
It's ok to want to be alone and still crave connection
Male? Female?
We exist on a spectrum of characteristics.
Hormones, tendencies that will evolve and grow
    as you get to know you more.
        quiet? loud?
        needy? independent?
        messy? tidy?
You never have to be just one thing
You are a complete and complex being that is ever
    growing, flowing, changing and evolving.
Like me, you are made up of the whole universe,
    everything
You bring worlds into being.

ACT

Actively plan something you could bring into being.
Do up the blueprints.
What conditions would be conducive for your
    Big Bang?
What do you need to add to your soil
    to make things grow?

MEDITATE

Before time, there wasn't so much a flow
    there was everything ... at the same time
Breathe deep
Life is messy
    everyone is complex
    many ideas existing at one time
We try to make sense of it all
Surrender
You don't have to understand it all to celebrate it all
Remember me
I am with you in the in between.

The Dakini remind us
to dance fiercely, to cut
free from whatever we,
desperately, cling to, and
reveal what we are
trying to hide.

I AM DAKINI

In Sanskrit my name means "to fly"
In Tibetan, "Sky goer"
I am ecstatic female energy;
celebrating the transitions between
    levels of awareness.
Some texts reveal me as a flesh-eating
    demoness under Kali,
I am also depicted as beautiful and joyful,
I represent the concept of liberation.
How you see me
    is how you see freedom.
Sometimes growth arrives veiled in garments
    of pain
Sometimes it is accompanied with joyful cries
    and dancing.
Through me, what you try to hide is revealed,

I usher you towards enlightenment and arouse
    blissful energy.
My home is the clouds
The music of the universe
My joy is the growth of those around me
Ecstatic and enlightened and enjoying every moment
I want this peace for you
    My rituals are dance
    Physical and ethereal
    Flying on updrafts
    Laughing bubbles
We were never meant to wallow
Our bodies are electric
We were made to jump and jolt
Illuminate and strike
I am there beside you.

REFLECT

Take a moment to
   reflect on the sensation within your body's joints
As your body unfurls, memories are released
Trauma finds its dwelling within the chambers of
   your frame
Releasing it carries a sting, a feral healing process
The burden of keeping trauma buried is
   a heavier weight to carry
Than the liberation found in its release,
   the act of repair.
It is during these raw moments, I dance,
Not to mock, but to reflect your radiance.
A midwife, reminding to breathe through the pain,
To reach the next level, where growth and
   freedom blend.

ACT

Find space to move
First stretch—feel all your muscle groups, stretch out
   your legs, hips, twist your back, your core, roll out
   your shoulders, lift your hands above your head.
Breathe deep.
Put music on or not, the joy will come from within,
   not outside you.
Spin, let your arms fly around you
Jump, twerk, silly dance
Dakini means to fly, I am the spirit that lifts you.

MEDITATE

This can be a more physical meditation
Your body remembering,
   feeling
   and working stuff out
   once you've spun and jumped
   you can keep standing or lie down and
   feel the earth below you,
   the air above you
Maybe everything is still spinning
I am all about that liberation
I am all around you
you are not alone.

Where Artemis asked for female companions and wished to remain virginal, pared down, Eos, in her rosy, insatiable lust for life, always wanted more. More light, more beauty, more men. Honour the simple cycles in life and the ostentatious as well.

I AM EOS

I am Goddess of the morning
Sister of Helios, the sun,
and Selene, the moon
Either pulled by my winged horses
or flying on my own wings
I bring in each day scattering the mist of night
for my brother to rise.
Each morning without fail
I leave my beautiful home in the dark and
Return home once my job is done
To rest for the day
They call me
Rosy-fingered and
Saffron-robed
My beauty is only rivaled
By the beauty of the morning sky
I am an artist in the first degree
Alpha Beauty
My home is delicious
Saffron incense

Saffron rice and rich spices
Delectable scents swimming through the air
Muslin veils flowing in the winds
Through the open windows and doors
Around my home
The early morning bird songs are
My music
The pool to keep me cool and relaxed
In my riverside home
my sanctuary
They say
I was cursed by Aphrodite—
I had seduced her lover Ares and as payback—
I was cursed to always be falling in love
With young mortals
What they call a curse I found lovely
To be "cursed" to always be falling in love
    doesn't have to be a curse.
I fall in love as often as I can
With the music that's playing
With the friends at my home
With the food in my belly

REFLECT

Fall in love
   as often as you can
With every movement of your beautiful body
Fall in love with every change in light
With every change in season
Fall in love, and when they deride your joy
Fall in love again
We should all be so lucky
Who are you in love with?
What do you love?
The beautiful thing about your heart is, it is always
   capable of more love.
How do you show your love?
I am Greek and we have eight types of love
   from our tradition:
   Eros (sexual passion)
   Philia (deep friendship)
   Ludus (playful love)
   Agape (love for everyone)
   Pragma (long standing love)
   Philautia (love of self)
   Storge (family love)
   Mania (obsessive love)
Reflect on these types and consider how
   they exist in your world?
What needs to be tended, what's out of balance?

MEDITATE

Open your eyes, look around you
Look inside, outside, and around. You are a miracle
The world around you is a miracle
The air in your lungs has been through the lungs of
   thousands of others. You are stardust
Remember me
Find a way to fall in love with everything around you
Think of the people who bring you pain
   find love for them
   think of the stresses in your life,
   find a way to love them
My love is with you.

Freya is the Queen and commander of Valkyries. She calls us to stand up and love ourselves. We are her kin. We are to arm ourselves to defend against limiting forces & dimiaishing thought s.

We have to protect our

Magick.

I AM FREYA

A Valkyrie and high priestess
I was the one who taught magic to Odin
    and the rest of the Aesir,
Before that, it was only the Vanir who
    practiced magic.
People forget these things
I was equal to Odin in the battle field,
He and I would divide the dead between who
    would go to Valhalla
 and who would go to Folkvangr, my domain.

Sessrúmnir is my home
In Asgard
My hall
The music playing airy and light
I am full of contradictions
The goddess of love and war
My hall is sturdy

My music light
My chariot strong
pulled by my two cats

I leave them wondering
Loki tells disgusting stories of me
And I respond with a twinkle in my eye
Loki accused me of turning my lover into a swine
    and riding him around in front of everyone-
I do have a boar, Hildisvini
I'll just keep smiling and waving
There is work to be done

Choose the battles worth fighting
Leave the rest
Those battles you choose
You fight to the death
And at death
I'll be there to take you to
Folkvangr
I am beside you.

REFLECT

What is the
    battle you are fighting right now?
Who is beside you?
What are your weapons?
Are you armed with a clear voice? Your gentle heart?
    your strong arms?
Are you looking out for the fallen around you?
Make sure to look out for those who have
    gone before you.
Honey and mead are very important to me, think of
    me when you make a toast or swirl some honey in
    your tea.

ACT

Whether it's writing a letter to a local councilor,
    joining a rally, or singing a song; fighting
    doesn't need to mean negatively aggressive, it can
    mean being passionately, actively spreading love
    and support.
What group aligns with your values? Can you
    support them?
What would you actively fight if you could? How
    could you take steps to do so?
How could you fight apathy? How could you fight
    inequality?
The trick is to begin in your own home, on your own
    block, do the work and keep going; relentlessly.

MEDITATE

Associated with me are amber, moonstone,
    rose quartz, garnet, amethyst
Friday is my day, burn essential oils: lime, lemon,
    jasmine. Find a space to relax your mind and your
    heart. Lay your weapons down
Breathe deep
    relax your muscles
    think about the battles in your life
    lay them down. Which battles serve you?
    Which battles eat energy? Which battles feed you?
Remember me
Collect your armour around you.
    You have an army at your side.

Gaia, where would we be without Gaia? She is the Earth, all loving, nuturing, intelligent cosmic force. Remember, your food is sacred nourishment, your shelter and clothes come from her and are blessed. We are just part of her divine garden.

❀

Gaia

I AM GAIA

Mother Nature
Fantastic Flora and Fauna
Green electricity
Throbbing life
Nature's Alpha
Primordial elemental
Source
When you walk through a garden
I am there
Highest mountain
Deepest ocean
When you breathe fresh air
I am with you
The cotton in your clothes
I hold you
The vegetables on your plate
I nourish you
The wood that frames your home
I shelter you

My home is lush greenery
Water flowing through
The mists, my carpets
I take care of my pets,
every creature is my ward
Everything in balance
Bees and birds are my music
Every morning
My ritual is to pronounce my gratitude
Throughout the day as I feel flashes of
Gratitude, I say it out loud
With ecstatic enthusiasm
And joy in my heart
Sometimes I create new things
Out of this gratitude
Poems
Books
Scarves
Soup
Bread
Filled with gratitude.

REFLECT

What are
    your creations?
What have you made?
What are you planning to create?
How do you protect your creations?
How do you create a safe space for your creations? a
    space where your creations are valued?
What are you grateful for?

ACT

Create something; bake a cake, make dinner, paint,
    sing a new song, move in a new way, create
    a sculpture out of clay, create a videogame or
    character...
Give thanks every day for the
Creations around you
For the ingredients we have around us
For our mind and our spirit
And the vision it takes to see what does not exist yet

MEDITATE

Prehnite
Is my stone
We are made in the image of the creator.
We are creators ourselves.

Our purpose is to create, to add to creation.
It doesn't need to be a human life, it can be
    a crochet doily.
Breathe deep
You are a goddess
What would you like to see in this world that
    doesn't exist yet?
    see it
    feel it
How does it exist in this world?
How does it affect this world?
Think of me
I am your sister

Hecate, goddess of the crossroads, reminds us of the magic within us. The Queen Witch reminds us not to fear the darkness around us or within us.

ecate

I AM HECATE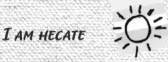

The goddess of magic,
    witchcraft, the night,
    the moon,
    ghosts and necromancy
I am the triple goddess
    Mother, Maiden, Crone
    Past, Present, Future
I am of the Underworld and
still bursting full of light
I helped Demeter find
    Persephone in the
    darkness of hell
    with just the torch
    of my heart
I am the protectress of
    households and entryways
I am a healer of the conflicts
    of the inner world

Goddess of the Crossroads
Sometimes my three heads are
    a dog, a snake and
    a horse
People leave offerings to me
    at the intersections where
    three roads meet
I understand the darkness is
    just the other half
The underside of a weaving
    and nothing to be feared
I heal and soothe fear.
My home is dimly lit
Dark curtains
Heavy fabrics
Candles

Black storax is my incense
Laurel and Saffron too,
fire in the hearth
Ancient heat from the fire
    of the beginning of time
Owls hooting, the buzz of
    fireflies buzzing
The flap of bat wings
The sounds of darkness are
    my soundtrack
Violins, cat gut strings
Howling songs of longing
I am a trickster and
    a true friend
I give you what you need
Not necessarily what
    you want
I am with you in the dark.

REFLECT

What are you
    afraid of?
What is it that frightens you? Why?
What do you avoid because it makes you
    uncomfortable?
What spaces in your life need clearing?
What crossroads do you find yourself at?

ACT

Take up a brave torch and look at your fear.
What is the source?
How bad could things be if the worst possibility
    happened? Death?
Death isn't the end, it's just the other half of life
How great could it be if the best happened?
What can you do each day to chip at your fear?

MEDITATE

Pearl, Ruby, Obsidian
Sit in a doorway.
In between, halfway up the stairs, like Robin
    the Frog from the Muppets.
When you are in between, settle in
Like the Baba Yaga

I won't always be there
    to make things easy
Sometimes you have to be at the end of your rope
Arrogance will push me to trickster
come as you are and contemplate your life
Breathe deep
    what crossroads are you at?
    what decisions need to be made?
Remember me
I thrive in the darkness and the half light,
    in the doorways and will always be
        there with a torch.

Inanna is ancient. Tribes have split and names have changed but she is still the goddess of sex and war.

Times will change and you will grow but always remember your roots.

nanna

I AM INANNA

I have many names
"Eldest daughter of the Moon"
"Lady of the Largest Heart"
   Ishtar
   Anahita
   Astarte
   Ostara
   Eostre
Sumerian Goddess venerated
   by the people of Uruk
My story begins 2000 years BC
And continues today
The first poems written were written to me
   from my loving priestess.
Cuneiform, on wet, clay tablets
   smashed as temples were looted and destroyed
   time and time again by different groups
   then unearthed, and rediscovered
My story, a jigsaw puzzle for the ages
A lover, a warrior queen, a blood-thirsty tyrant
   and a loving moon goddess,
     giving of the gift of knowledge and
     understanding
I was the beginning, as people shifted and
   language changed so did my name:

Inanna with the Sumerians, Ishtar with the Akkadians, Babylonians, Assyrians, then Anahita with the rise of the Persians, Saraswati in Hindu, Astarte with the Phoenicians, Aphrodite with the Greeks and Venus with the Romans.

My stories connect with many of our more contemporary stories: I descend to the depths of the underworld to save my love, at each gateway gifting a garment or piece of jewellery. By the time I enter the underworld, I am naked. Armed with all my grandeur at the beginning of my trek, I enter into the heart of the underworld with nothing but my bare self.

This resonates with the story of Salome, who drops her veils and reveals truths. In the underworld, I am hung on a tree for insolence and hang for three days. My companion makes the journey back up to heaven to get help for me, but the gods are unhappy I went on the journey and it takes time to gather aid. I am resurrected in three days time, reminiscent of the resurrection patterns of familiar stories.

REFLECT

Where is the
   source of your origin story? Dig back,
   names are temporary, they change with the one
   writing the story
Who are you?
How did you get here?
What civilizations rose and fell
   and how did you make it here?
Reflect on your roots.

ACT

Write a poem to your governing queen,
   no matter who she is
Think about your values, your super powers
   and seek out the one who rules over these entities
I am connected to the Dog Star Sirius
   who is the bringer of the flood season
Later I connect to the planet Venus
The brightest entity in the sky besides the sun.
I am the illumination, knowledge, brilliance
What are your associations?

MEDITATE

Lapis Lazuli is my stone
At night, when the crescent moon hangs in the sky,
   that's me in my moon-shaped boat

Sit comfortably
Breathe deep
Remember who you are
Regardless of the languages and
   words changing
Who are you?
See yourself in all your glory
   your armour,
   your wealth
   and as you peel those things back
Remember me standing naked
   in front of the gates of hell
Know that you have everything it takes inside you to
   accomplish anything.

43

Jezebel reminds us to watch our backs. When you are strong, beautiful and intelligent, weak people will fear you. They will slander your name and try to push you out of windows for dogs to eat.

I AM JEZABEL

I am a Phoenician
I worship Baal
If they didn't want me and my god
They should've left us alone
But of course I was a bargaining chip
I was a pawn in their game
They hate you when you play along
And they hate you when you don't
I was just doing right by my god
I was just doing what I felt was best
Who wrote my story?
I am now labeled the archetypal
   "wicked woman"
Men wrote the story
Again those monotheists
A pissing contest
Who's god is better?
My god is the god of nature

Who are we to Baal?
Human problems are nothing
   in the lives of gods
How many lives lost?
And for what?
They brag about throwing me out the window
Because of my red lipstick?
Because I was outspoken?
They brag about the dogs that ate me
Big brave men

I am Alpha Woman
Goddess of self-confidence
Straightforwardness
Strategy
Scheming
Call on me when you have
Something to get done

REFLECT

Reflect on a time when people misunderstood you
Used you
Ended up hating you for
Your role in their disaster
Feel all the feelings that come
    from these moments
You gave your power to someone else
Someone who wasn't ready to take care of it
Don't listen to the stories they tell about you
You know you
You don't need to convince anyone else
Truth is essential
Truth is timeless
Truth feels really good

ACT

Take out your red lipstick
Put it on, or at least have it beside you
Write down your pride
Write down your excitement
Your joy, your peace and your truth
Write a mantra for your self
Who you are
Who you strive to be
End with hope

MEDITATE

Sit comfortably. Somewhere you feel you can be safe
Back straight head high. You're a queen
Breathe slow and deep
Let the air slide into every part of your lungs
Feel the oxygen in your veins
In every part of you. Your toes, your legs
Your belly. Your arms and your fingers and your
everything. Slow down
Exhale all the negativity
Breathe in your truth. The light.
    Beauty. Power. Good Energy
The dogs won't get you today.

Kali reminds us that we could rip their arms off and add them to our arm skirt if we wanted to. Remember that once you have decimated your foes to dance with vim and vigor over their corpses, and you can always bring them back to life if you choose.

I AM KALI

I was once an old crone
But I'm younger now, easier to be around
Blue skinned and smiling
Tongue lolling
Twinkle in my eye, big hips swaying
I have a skirt made from the arms of my foes
And I have a necklace of heads
Bloodlust or tantric creativity ...
      You decide
I have a temper, Alpha rage
They tell you anger is a bad thing
It's a doorway

I am the shadow work
I do not shy away from conflict, or pain
My home is a gambling house
A Tavern
A Slaughter House
Wrapped in ill-gotten gold
Dancing all the while
Don't expect me to vacuum the carpets

If you come to visit
You can smell blood in the air
    Smoke
    Sweat
    Salted meat
    Rich spices, Nag champa incense
    Burning
I am all the smells that make your
Heart race
    Hard liquor
    Saliva
    Cigars
You dare think you can sacrifice something to me and
    I'll be appeased?
I'll do what you want me to do?
No
That's not how this works
Don't let people expect things of you
Keep them on their toes
Sure, sometimes I go too far
I can fix what I need to
But it's important to be self determined
And free.

REFLECT

These are my stones
   Black tourmaline
   Smoky quartz
   Garnet
   Labradorite
Have them around you and reflect
Do you give and find yourself being
   Resented
These are the six stages of what can happen
If you are in a one-way
   giving relationship or situation:
Appreciation, Anticipation, Expectation
Entitlement, Dependency, Resentment
Reflect on the relationships in your life
Are they two-way relationships?
Are you being appreciated for the work you do?

ACT

Shadow work
Think about your triggers
Things that anger you
Things that spark rage
Ask yourself why these things bring you anger
What parts of yourself do you hide?
Shadow work needs you to be honest with yourself.
There's nothing wrong with having a shadow.

MEDITATION

Lion's breath practice is all about loosening up your
   creativity, your voice, and banishing rage
Sit and lean forward comfortably
Rest your front paws gently on your knees or the floor
   in front of you. Spread your claws
Inhale through your nose
Open your mouth wide, stick out your tongue, stretch
   it down towards your chin
Exhale forcefully. While exhaling make a "ha"
   sound from deep in your abdomen
Breathe normally for a few moments
Repeat lions breath up to seven times.

La Loba reminds us that everything must die, but that's not the end. We must gather remains around us, learn the songs of the dead and sing to them. In that moment of song, the once dead will be resurrected and leave us, so the process will begin again. Creation is a cycle not a straight line.

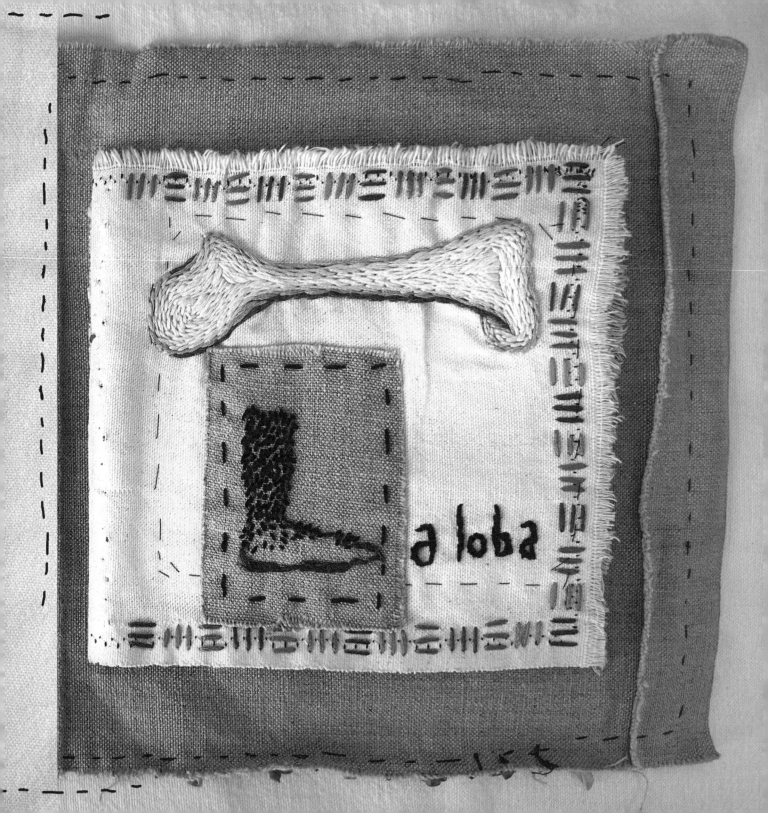

I AM LA LOBA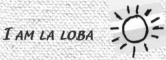

Wolf Woman
A solitary crone
Living in the caves of the desert
Lit by fat candles at night
And the sun in the day
I am hairy and lumpy
   difficult to decipher between
   animal and human
Most days
My back is curled to
See the earth
Find the bones
My cave is a plethora
An assortment of small and large
Bleached white bones
I love the wolf bones
The best
I lay them out
In exact and intuitive perfection

Once full and complete
I sit with this
   white-lace sculpture
And get to know it
Which song does it know
   and need?
The sounds are guttural
Not porcelain but gristle
And I sing
And the wolves in
   the hills sing
   with me
   in the night
And flesh returns
To the bones
And the fur comes
   next
And the tail swishes
With love
And then it breathes in
And runs

I am on the lookout for that
Which is in danger of
Disappearing
In this world
We must
Preserve the
Delicate creatures
The threatened creatures
The ones forgotten
I am bone woman
I am the thing of myths
From many different peoples
I am the circle of life
Remember
Death is not the end
Time is not a line
We are a connected interwoven
Wreath
I will sing over you
And you will sing over me
Life will go on.

REFLECTION

When we think about loss in our lives
Reflect on how we feel. Helpless? Alone?
Remember those losses live on in our hearts
We keep them alive in our hearts and actions
Lay out the bones of those who have gone
    Photographs, Knick knacks, Stories
And remember the Songs
Draw out the bones if the bones aren't there
Life is not a one way ticket
We are forever looping through others consciousness
And they through us
You are not alone.

ACT

The thoughts in our heads are bones
The feelings in our hearts are bones
The songs that float through our lips and our skin
    are bones
Lay out those bones and bring them back
This can take place anywhere
You may be on the bus
And a song might remind you of a friend
Sit there with them. This is work
Shadow work that some shy away from
Go past the pain of loss and sit with your friend.

MEDITATE

Sit and breathe. If you make sounds make sounds
Let them come out. From your belly
From your rage of loss
From your sadness, from your joy
Hum, and breathe
And exist in a moment
With everyone
Together with you
You are not alone
We are made up of those who have gone before
Breathe
I am with you.

Mary reminds us to love,
through pain and loss, love,
believe in that LOVE.

I AM MARY

I am Mary
   the Mother
I am grace and compassion
Personified
Humility and patience
Some say I was
   Christianity's answer
To the old Mother goddesses
Before me: Athena, Artemis,
   Diana, Gaia, Isis
Virginal and holy
I try to do each of them justice
   in my turn
I am brave, I am peaceful
And I am full of love
Full of forgiveness and gentleness
I risked my life to have my son,
   guide him and stand by him
Some people call me crazy
Don't they always?

When you have something
   driving you
That they don't understand?
I was always different
As a child I was quiet,
   reserved
Only took what I needed
Lived in monasteries
Wove fine fabrics
Virginal weaves
Pure movements
I have always
   appreciated calm
Quiet
Gentle breezes through
   open windows
Laundry hanging on lines
Whites
Blues
My home is a retreat from
   the chaos of life
The rage of masses

I pray as often as I can
My life is a prayer
The rhythm of the weaving
Meditation
The water while cleaning
   Hymns
Singing while handing out food
   Psalms
Each footstep a letter to Creator
I had to overcome my pain
You will have to overcome
   your pain
Life moves on in
   slow thoughtful moments
And that loss never goes
But neither do your loved ones
They are with you
And you keep walking forward
   In their honour
   With grace, and quiet
   And peace
I am with you.

REFLECT

What have you lost? What have you gained?
Sit with your pain and consider the lessons
Each stab to your heart
Reveals something
Release the flow of something new
There is no shame in pain or loss
They will reframe how you see everything
How do you see your world now?
Do you see the pain in others' eyes?
Do you help comfort those around you?
Love Yourself
   Those in need
   Those who come to you
   And those who don't
I am with you when you feel weak.

ACT

As an act of defiance
To fight that urge to hide yourself away
Give something away
Maybe your time, maybe your gifts
Create something and gift it to someone in need
Your time is a gift. You are a gift
Everyone around you benefits when you open up.

MEDITATE

Find a quiet place, light a white candle
Breathe deep. Witness mothers who have gone before
Feel the weight of their sacrifice, hard work, and love
Say a thank you for these lessons
Don't forget these acts of love
Appreciate all you do for those around you
You are that light for someone in your life
Feel that light of love inside you, let it radiate out
Keep that feeling with you
Remember to radiate the light when life gets hard
Keep that fire burning.

Na'asjéii Asdzáá, Grand mother spider is always near, when we need guidance or protection. Through journeys and adventures and tests and trials, between worlds, deep into the lower river, she is there.

I AM NA'ASHJÉ'II ASDZÁÁ

Grandmother spider
Navajo protectress
Spinning webs of stories
And of love
Weaving shields of protection
I have been here since the
    beginning
To help the humans
I live in the caves
In the river below
I exist in the darkness and
When you are in trouble I will be
    there
I know my way to the light
I know what you will need
It may be a blanket
Or a tourniquet

You may need a spool of
    thread to help
You out of a labyrinth
Or a yarn to weave a baby
    wrapping
I have the knowledge of
    the earth and the deep
    crevices and caverns
The shadows and the deep
    spaces
I am alpha weaver
My home is full of rich
    fabrics
Warmth in a cool place
I have the fire of the center
    of the earth burning
    always
Coal from the beginning of
days

You can't lose that fire
Never let that fire go out
You are never alone
I am never far
In the upside down
In between
The trick is to remember you can
    ask questions
You can ask for help
Make a loving home
Fill it with beginning of time love
Remind those around you they can
    always come to you for help
To this first fire
To this place of acceptance
No judgment
No harsh words
A place of guidance
And inner light.

REFLECT

Who do you
    go to for
    for guidance
Reflect on all the people in your life
Who is there with non-judgment
And an open heart?
Who wants the best for you
Wanting nothing in return?
Appreciate that person
Make sure you show your appreciation to these people
    in your life
Are you that person for people?
How can you settle into non-judgment?

ACT

Write a letter of appreciation
    to someone in your life who is
    a shining light of non-judgment
Deliver it
It can be anonymous or signed
The point is to say thank you
And I see you
To someone who rarely is acknowledged
For their subtle but powerful kindness.

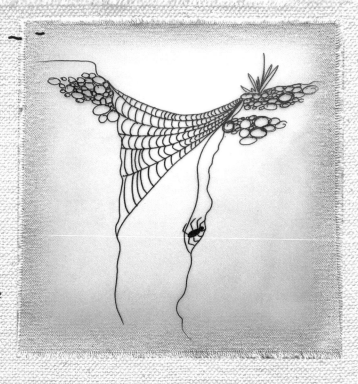

MEDITATE

Relax and imagine your eyes seeing the good in the
    world around you
Imagine your nose
Breathing the goodness of the world around
Imagine your ears, only hearing kindness
Imagine your mouth in your minds eye
Only saying words of love
Imagine your heart, relax that big muscle
Only feel love and softness
Let the hardness crumble
Breathe deep, I am with you.

O Erdo ben, She of the Woods
reminds us of the wilderness
within us. We are FREE.

I AM Ő ERDŐBEN

She of the Woods
Long hair
Rough skin
No shoes
Claws that scratch the earth
As I walk
I drag my toes
And plant wildflowers
    in the grooves
My home is the forest
Alpha flora
My music is the song birds
My companions
The other forest folk
The lost
The lonely
The bugs

And the things that eat the bugs
I make my own clothes
Skins stitched together
Sinew and twine
I have no more than I need
I move around
Like the wind
Like the rain clouds
I am here to remind you
You are free
You have to fight for your freedom
There are things and objects and stuff
That will clog up your air
Cover your surfaces
Stop you from breathing
Know what gives you life and what
    takes it away.

REFLECT

Reflect on where you live
How do you feel about your home?
Take stock of what makes you feel good and
    what makes you feel anxiety
Is it as simple as the laundry needs to be done?
Or is it bigger, do things need to be moved,
    or thrown out?
Sit, don't rush or act rashly
But feel deeply, intentionally
Not just the things in your home but the home itself
We forget we've made choices to get where we are
Priorities and jobs and obligations have placed us
    where we are now. Are you happy?
Remember, you are free, we are free
You have all of nature inside you
Can you reconcile your insides with your outsides?
For peace?

ACT

Clean your house
Organize your things and
    donate what you don't need
Fresh and clean spaces
Open windows
You need air.

MEDITATE

Open your windows
Sit on a clean floor, comfortably
Imagine trees all around you
I am She of the woods, my home is in the trees
Scent of pine, Cedar, Oak
Imagine with your mind's eye
Your roots reaching deep into the earth
Drawing the energy from Mother Earth
Giving your own energy back
A fluid transaction, reciprocity
I am with you in this exchange
You are free.

Persephone celebrates both the light and darkness. The Queen of the Underworld and of Springtime. There is a time to mourn and a time to glow with new life.

I AM PERSEPHONE

Queen of the Underworld
Hades' consort
I am so much more than that
The goddess of fertility and life
I am the reason for spring
And winter
New life and death
Light and Darkness
Joy and sorrow
I have the white dresses,
The greens and blues for the
    springtime
And I have the black gowns
The blood reds
For the dark times,
Winter
My life is split
Between the beauty and
    the peace
Of Greece in springtime

And the macabre divinity of
The underworld in winter.
My home in Greece is the
    home of Demeter and
    Zeus
Royal
Fertile
Bursting with life
Flowers, fruits, orchards,
    children
Laughter and music
Singing and flutes
Wheat is my symbol
And so is the pomegranate
My home in the Underworld
Is deliciously decorated
With deep crimsons and
    indigos
Minor chords and nocturnes
Play on the gramophone

While skeletons dance
When the darkness comes
    remember,
A weaving has two sides
Two sides of the same tapestry
The positive and the flipped
    negative
Day will come
And the trick is to not wish the
    night away
Find solace in the darkness
Rest Recharge
Use different muscles
Take time for activities
    of the dark
And then, when spring comes
Or morning
The shift will be refreshing
You'll be ready
And I'll be there with you.

REFLECT

Reflect on what
  you do in the different times of year
Do you celebrate each moment?
Do you dread a particular season? Why?
See if you can shift your thoughts
Can you find beauty or divinity in
That which you view with trepidation?
Can you find a new hobby or something to look
  forward to
Even in your least favorite time of year? Maybe
  eventually, each day will be a joy to behold, to
  take part in
You're on your path.

ACT

When you wake up in the morning
You are in the land of the living
Being able to walk amongst the gods
So walk, and dance
And sow seeds
And harvest beautiful creations
And while you live
Live
And go to sleep each night
In awe of the day
And grateful for the night.

MEDITATE

Sit or stand comfortably
Hands over your heart, at your sides or on your knees
Breathe in deep, breathe in life
The possibilities that today brings
Breathe out the regrets, the sadnesses
Bring your arms up skyward as you
Breathe in, reach up as far as you can
And gently and slowly as you breathe out
Roll down and reach earthwards, comfortably
Breathe in, straighten your back, and rest
This is your way home back to your center
I am with you, in dark and light.

The Qallupilluk remind us why we tell stories. Sometimes there needs to be a monster lurking under the ice to save the lives of the children.

I AM QALLUPILLUK

Green scaly skin
That keeps me warm in the
   Frigid oceanic waters
   Just below the ice
The Inuit tell stories of me
Warn your children

Long fingernails
Stringy hair
Duck skin clothes
Big sack on my back
   for the children
   that get too close to the edge

When you hear the water knocking
   against the underside of the ice
When you smell sulfur
When the ice is cracking in spring
I am there

Some say I love the taste
   of children
Some say I can't have
   children of my own
And take the local kids to
   raise as my own

Either way,
   whatever you hear
Whatever you believe
The truth stands
There needs to be warning
   stories to tell children
Stories that will make sense
   to children
To keep them safe

Humans are good storytellers
Stories serve many purposes
To enrapture, to console
To inspire, and to warn

Stories are woven through
   human history
You cannot separate the story
   and people
Be it spoken or written
The word has always been there
Even when it was an image

I am Qallupilluk
Alpha teacher
I'll be the monster
So you can keep
   your children safe.

REFLECT

Are there warnings that people should get
When preparing to deal with you?
Is there a sound that declares your entrance?
The tinkling of bells?
The slashing of chefs knives?
Humming?
Are there smells that herald your arrival?
Maybe lavender? Sandalwood?
Sweat?
Humans and stories have a long history
A history that has purpose and
Importance and reason
Stories are not frivolous
Nursery rhymes and children's games too
They were created to teach
Inuit knew the dangers of the shifting spring ice
And they the knew the curiosity of their children
I am the reason to not get too close.

ACT

Write a fairy tale or a
    mythology that incorporates you
What would it be about?
Would it be a warning tale?
Would it be a heroic tale of inspiration?

MEDITATE

Lie down on the floor
Or maybe in the bath
Breathe deep
This existence is about more than you
What great purpose do you serve
Big picture
Are you here
    to teach people softness?
Are you here
    to teach people gratitude?
Or steadfast love?
Meditate on what you are to other people
And what lessons your very existence teaches.

Rhiannon, the White Witch,
the Welsh Horse Goddess,
She reminds us to create.
To sing songs that have never
been heard before, write words
that will never again be
written and paint images that
are in your heart alone.

Phiannon

I AM RHIANNON

I am a moon goddess
A horse goddess
A goddess of loyalty and of
    forgiveness
Of creativity
My home is in Wales
I am queen of the fairies
And queen of Dyfed
    with my king Pwyll
I have white roses in my house
    in vases
And hanging in the corners of the
    rooms, drying
And growing throughout my garden
Golden threads shine in my pillows
    and dresses and in my hair
Reminiscent of the glow
    of the moon
And the warmth of my heart
I have music always playing and
Tunes always on my lips
Toes always dancing
    and tapping

Poems always spilling from
    my fingers
I have been loved so richly
    by my husband
I have been betrayed by my
    maids
And I have worked hard
Tirelessly
To show my true character
I am goddess of horses
Not only for the raw beauty
    and demure grace of the
    creatures
But also in honour of
    their strength
I have been known as
    a giantess
A foreboding woman of
    immense tenacity
And this is how it goes
Live in such a way that
    no one would bear false
    witness against you
And if they do
If the situation is so grave

and so ugly that even those
    who love you, tell lies
Live in such a way that no one
    believes those lies
And have faith that the truth
    will show itself
And marinate so completely
    in grace that
Forgiveness isn't even a choice
It's a given
This is the feeling one feels while
    looking at the full moon on a
    still night
Or when you witness an awe-
    inspiring creature at full tilt
    in all its majesty
This is it
Grace
With the tunes of song birds on
    the breeze
And delicate flow of golden lace
    in the open windows
Breathe deep
You are on the right path.

REFLECT

What are you doing to cultivate grace in your heart?
The practice of forgiveness is complex and nuanced
It walks hand in hand with the practice of creating
Grace could be likened to creating a soft space
A space where you are safe to be you
Do your best and be patient with yourself
If we can create this soft space for ourselves
    and keep it in earnest
We can begin to let others into the soft space
The more we practice keeping that space
The larger that space will grow until
    we are all able to exist in this beautiful kingdom.

ACT

Sing a song, maybe it's a song you know
 Maybe it's a song you just started singing when
    someone asked you a question and you felt the
    excitement to respond in melody
Or maybe you're by yourself and you're talking to
    yourself in song
Maybe it's a song to the moon
Maybe it sounds like howling
Maybe your pain is coming out like whimpering but
    you turn it into a somber tune
Music is grace.

MEDITATE

Sit comfortably. Breathe deep. Feel the breath go in
Reaching all the deep crevices of you
When you go to breathe out, hum the breath out
As you breathe back in, imagine your inner world
The space where you are creating grace
Hum the breath out
When thoughts come, let them pass through. Keep
    focusing on your breath and your humming and
    your inner space
This is a path back to you
A way to find your way home
Coming back to your core, your joy and your peace.

Sekhmet is the daughter of Ra. She is both a wild tyrant and a healer. She is not worried about going to extremes. She is not moderate. Lady of Pestilence and Terror and Lady of Life reminds us that we need not be moderate.

I AM SEKHMET

The daughter of Ra
Or rather "The Eye of Ra"
Lion-headed woman
I am who Ra sent to remind
    the humans
Who was in charge
You've heard the story before
The humans begin to act in
    a deplorable fashion
Ra is upset and needs someone
    to straighten them out
Instead of a flood
I rained destruction of
    another kind
I became blood thirsty
My deeds began to turn even
    Ra's stomach
He called me off but I
    couldn't stop

It took gallons of beer
Made to look like blood
Dyed with pomegranate juice
to slow me down
And I slept
And my blood thirst
Dissipated
Like the darkness
The light came
And I carried on
Moderation is more
    comfortable
Rarely do you find friends
    who can accept
Extremes

If you can find someone
    who sees the
Beauty in your wild nature

Value their friendship
Have a glass of wine
Or red tea
Light a fire
And hold red stones near

Delight in the extremes
    of the seasons
And nurture those
    around you too
To do the same
Delight in extremes
In the emotions that
    surface and
In the physical responses
When you are ill
Feel all that illness entails
And when you are healthy
Revel in your body.

REFLECT

Reflect on your friendships and allies
Reflect on your spaces
Are you able to stretch
Are you able to be you
Bring all your gifts to the table?
Do you find yourself hiding aspects of yourself
    around certain people?

ACT

Write down the aspects of you
That you are afraid to show
-If there are any-
Are there people in your life who know and
    celebrate these aspects?
Are they hidden from everyone?
Humans are complex beings and you are
    made up of many different gifts
And you are constantly evolving
And the world is constantly shifting
Look at characteristics of yourself regularly
And reflect on what is valued and what is hidden
    This can be done maybe yearly? Or more
When you need it
When you feel the need to be seen.

MEDITATE

Say your name out loud. "I am..."
Names are important
Some of us have chosen our own names
Some of us have grown into our names
Some of us have secret names
I am .... Breathe deep
Think of all the things that name conjures
I am the Lady of Pestilence ... and the Lady of Life
Do people have different names for you?x
Breathe deep and repeat your name out loud
This is one step closer to coming home
I am with you.

Tanit is Baal's consort. Highly
revered in Carthage, she reminds
us that we have no right to
speak for the dead or for long passed
deities. Was the burial ground in her
name one of 20 000 children who
were burned alive in sacrifice to a blood
thirsty witch or was it a site to bring
still born, miscarried and young children
so they could be returned to a loving
mother figure in their after life?

I AM TANIT

A reminder that
We do not speak for the dead
No matter the clues
If you weren't there
If you didn't speak to the artist or
If you didn't live in that area
You couldn't possibly know

There are so many narratives driven by fear
So many stories repeated out of envy
Or gossip mongering

Ugly qualities in famous figures
    are glorified
Sometimes beautiful qualities are embellished
    when dealing with heinous characters
People pull what they want and magnify these
    qualities when they choose

I am Tanit
I am an old goddess
Consort to an old god
TNT with no vowels originally used
the pronunciation shifts
I am closely related to Astarte
Or Ishtar. Or Inanna
We are all connected
as the people shifted
We became what they needed us to be
Like Sekhmet I am from time to time
Lion-headed

Remnants of olive tree branches were
    found at my tophet
When you use olive oil think of me
Think of mother's fire
Think of warmth
Think of home.

REFLECT

Reflect on your time and your culture
Imagine you are from another place
Another time altogether and you
Dig up the remains from your home
What values are important in your culture?
What ideas do you hold dear?
Would those be obvious through your
　　material possessions?
If your things were dug up
In an archeological site
What would be discovered about you?
What stories would be written about
your belongings left behind?

ACT

Consciously buy things that
　　reflect your values
Your money speaks to the world
　　about what you believe in
The things you own
Whether you like it or
　　not reflect who you are.

MEDITATE

Sit in a quiet and safe place
Light a white candle
This is reminiscent of the moon
Have something blue around, this is a colour of Tanit
When you tell stories,
　　reflect on which stories are yours to tell
Breathe deep and reflect on a clear quartz,
　　be transparent in your actions and deeds, do not
　　tell stories that aren't yours to tell
Spread love and honesty and encourage others
　　to do the same.

Urania, the muse of astrology. Where her 8 sisters focused on earthly arts, music, poetry, chorus, Urania looked to the heavens. Don't be afraid to look around and ponder the skies.

rania

I AM URANIA

I can tell the future
From the arrangement
   of the stars
And can tell the past
by the look in your eyes
I wear a gorgeous blue cloak
   with stars embroidered on it
And wear lavender perfume
I am the muse of night
My eyes to the celestial heights
I don't wake when everyone
   else wakes
I hold my own hours
Like the owls
And the bats
The wolves
My sisters are the other muses
And are concerned with the arts
Of the earth
Of day time

And afternoon time
And evening
Calliope, Clio, Erato,
   Euterpe, Melpomene,
   Polyhymnia, Thalia,
   Terpsichore
Epic poetry, choral and
   instrumental music
Theatre, tragic and comic,
   romantic poetry,
   creativity
I am concerned with the
   connection of the stars
   and their stories
   to our stories.
We are made from
   the stardust
We are woven from
   thousand year old
   remnants
Bits from here and there
and

Our actions are echoes of
Sounds that have gone before
I tie those loose ends together
   to tell those stories
I have mathematical tools
And my equations
I pull from all the corners
I'm not limited to romantic
   glances at twinkling lights
My flower is the
   Night-Blooming Cereus
Those of the day will miss
The blooms of this mystical
   flower and meteor showers
The aurora borealis
When the daily grind
Is wearing you down
Get quiet and calm and when
   the darkness spreads
Look up
I am there
Alpha stargazer.

REFLECT

When was the last time you got out to the darkness
    and looked up?
Maybe you live in the country
And stars are your nighttime brethren
But if you live in the city
You might forget the magic of the stars
Maybe you see the moons changes and
    you witness the planets
And maybe the glow of the streetlights
    appease some kind of primal connection
    to the stars
But every once in a while
Take a drive.

ACT

Take a drive out to the darkness
Maybe bring a friend
Shared magic is double magic
Also safety
But to be in the darkness
To look up and see the
    Pinholes
The sparkling threads of the heavens
I am there looking up.

MEDITATE

Wait until the sun goes down
Light your favorite incense
Imagine all the stars surrounding you
You are among the stars
If you've read "The Little Prince"
Imagine birds carrying you through the planets
Among the stars
Who do you see?
What stories do you remember?
Safe travels
I am with you in the stars.

Venus, the goddess of love,
sex, fertility and beauty.
Botticelli immortalized her
in a scallop shell, hair blown
about by Zephyr and Aura.
Perfection. You are perfect.

♡

I AM VENUS

Goddess of love
Of beauty and sensuous delight
When you witness me in the scallop shell
You can smell the sea spray
That salty oceanic olfactory delight

I am the beauty that came from the
Ugliness of Saturn castrating Uranus
From that saltiness
I am the sweetness

I am the sweetness of longing and
Of feeling loved
And nurtured
Feeling it in your nerves
And feeling it in your bones
All your senses are heightened

Let the wind play in your hair
Zephyr and Aura
The wind gusts and the breezes
Will guide you on your journey
They will deliver you to your shore
Let each season wrap you in a cloak of love
No matter where you come from
You are perfect
You were created for a reason
You are exactly where you were meant to be
Revel in each moment

Each of us in our space and time
Are manifestations of love
Let it radiate outwards from you
You are perfect

I am Venus
Alpha love.

REFLECT

Think about a
    time when you felt out of place
Maybe you blew in from a different country
Or maybe you started a new career
And you feel like an outsider
Or maybe you just always associate with the
    identity of outsider
Maybe you're used to not fitting in
Remember Venus in her perfect
Sea shell
A pearl of loveliness arriving on the banks
She was out of place too
Own it.

ACT

Cook or bake with Cinnamon
Cinnamon is my spice
Lovely. Sultry. Can be used for dinner and dessert!
Find a recipe and take time to think about me
In all my grandeur
Whether it's a bursting forth of life from the quiet
    of winter or a celebration of harvest and a
    settling in to the darkness
You are my family
How could you be anything but perfect?

MEDITATE

Light an oceanic candle
Hold a seashell
The flow of the waves
The winds. The smells
Breathe in deeply. Breathe in life
Breathe in turmoil
And serenity
And grit and cleanliness
You are renewed
Born again
I am with you.

Wuriupranili never tires of the routine.
Every morning she lights her
stringy bark torch and dusts herself
with red ochre. As she ascends
she dusts the clouds with her colour.
She begins in the east and after
spanning the sky settles in the west
where she redecorates herself in
ochre and flourishes once more before
heading to her subterranean tunnel
to get ready for her curtain call in the
east the next morning.

I AM WURIUPRANILI

Sun Woman
I reside in Australian folklore
In the sky and in the earth below
A constant flow of bringing light
And carrying my ember
In my underground tunnel to get
To my starting point again

I don't sleep
But I do shift gears
I go from full glory across the sky to
Dormant
    whispering

There will be times in your life
When you need to keep moving
Forward always
Not slowing pace or stopping

And that's okay

As long as you make a shift

Maybe it's teaching in the day
And painting or writing at night
Maybe it's working for a year
And taking a year to go to
School
Even if you don't sleep
You need to shift

Sometimes you'll be flaming
And bright and sometimes you'll be
Keeping the ember burning
In the dark
I am walking beside you
Alpha movement.

REFLECT

What do you do
   to shift gears?
A human is complex and in need
Of many different stimulus
You get dopamine from many sources
Try out different things to
Expand different parts of who you are.

ACT

When you are working so hard
Your hands are shaking
Your heart is getting weak
And you wonder how you continue to move
It is not necessarily sleep alone that is needed
Your soul needs rest too
You may get up from a beautiful slumber still tired
   and feel even more dejected
You need to create
You need to fill your soul back up
And that comes from making connections
With others and with yourself through your art
What is your art?
You may need to switch from art form to art form and
   find the right action that fills your heart
I am working beside you.

REFLECT

Find quiet and darkness
Maybe it's at the coming of the sun
Or maybe you are in nighttime mode
Carrying your ember in your heart
Breathe deeply
Breathe in all the calm around you
Breathe out slowly. Breathe out despair
Breathe in beauty
Breathe out desperation.
Breathe in excitement
You are alive and time is short.

Xihe was the mother of ten suns, each of them were three legged birds. Each morning, one of the suns had to rise, but one time, all ten suns ascended and the world began to burn. Houyi, the archer, shot all but one down and saved us all. Xihe reminds us of the power we hold within ourselves. She reminds us how to wield that power.

I AM XIHE

I live in my beautiful home in
    China
Mulberry trees abound
My ten suns were three legged
    crows
Who lived in the trees
Incense always burning
Music always playing
Things had to be serene at home
    because
The rest of life was so exhausting
I have a great duty
I drive the carriage across the sky
    each day
Carrying one of my suns

They were wild
And they longed to reach down to
    the earth
To eat from the immortal grasses

To take part in earthly
    delights
But they are the sun
And what they touch they
    scorch

So I was a wrangler
Of unruly young ones who
    longed to live life
Free of responsibilities

But we have responsibilities
We have immense power
And with that we have
    incredible responsibility

When my suns forgot that
    responsibility
One day
They all flew up and
All ten suns brought flames
    to the earth

Chaos
Destruction and death

Houyi was called for and
My suns
Were all shot down
One by one
With one left
I begged him to leave one so the
    people of Earth wouldn't have
    to live in darkness

You have incredible power within
    you
You have the power to build up
    and to bring life
And you have the power to destroy

Be a force of creation and love
I am with you
Driving your chariot
Shine.

REFLECT

What is your
   incredible gift?
What could happen if you let go
And let it run free?
I am Xihe and I am here to
Remind you that you are responsible for
Everything you create
You are responsible for how it's interpreted
And how it affects people
We have entered a time of empathy
Are we helping and healing?
Or are we hurting?
And how can we grow for next time?

ACT

Think about your actions
Your daily interactions. Your facial features
Your gut responses
Are you doing your best to scorch the least earth
   possible?
The world is an exhausting place
And to keep the beautiful music going
And the incense burning
In a manner of speaking
Be that peace for
   those around you.

MEDITATION

Light some incense at the coming of the sun
Remember what I lost and see my last sun
Rise. Close your eyes
Breathe deep. Breathe in peace
And gentleness
And cooling touch
And breathe out your fire
Breathe deep and when you breathe out
Let resentments go
Let them release their grip on your heart
Breathe in clean fresh air and breathe out pain
I am with you.

Yamuna, boundless love and passion, an overflowing. She is the largest tributary of the Ganges, in India and reminds us to be sources of boundless love.

I AM YAMUNA

I am the river
Ever changing
Ever the same
Ever flowing
I am pure and true
And the source of
Boundless life
And love

My home is in the Yamunotri Glacier
In northern India
Lush and delicious
People from all walks of life
Come to visit me as spring starts to shine
And the waters start to flow

And I accept all the visitors with
    loving open arms
Be an open palm
Accept all the love when the love is flowing
And be there to send it out when it's in need

I am pure compassion
There is a story that tells of my brother
Leaving the family to become the
    god of death
I cried and cried over the loss of him
and formed the river with my tears
And those tears of love and loss
Make it so
Whomsoever dips their toes into me
Will not have to endure a painful death
Many stories are told and
    many celebrations
Were created in my honour
Each of them with love and
    compassion at the root

Be the river true
Overflowing with love for your
brothers and sisters
I am with you and will fill you up
When you feel low.

REFLECT

When was the
   last time you gave something freely
Without wanting anything in return
Even a smile
For those with little there is a tendency
To want to hold on to what you have
For those with much
There can be a tendency to want more
Find your way to the sweet spot
In between
How can you have enough to sustain yourself and to
   help those around you
And I'm not speaking of material things
When your heart is open
And you realize we are connected
We realize it's our world
It's our laughter
And our tears
You begin to flow

ACT

Find a river
Sit safely beside it
Close your eyes and listen to the water flow
This is life.

MEDITATE

Listen to the river in your heart
Don't forget that your
Heart carries with it a river
You are flowing inside
Get quiet and listen to the river in your heart
Breathe in slowly and quietly
Feel the blood flowing within you
Breathe out slowly and quietly
Each time slowing down to really focus on the
Flow
I am with you. You are home.

The Zorya Sisters, the morning star, the midday star and the evening star. Three sisters that must watch the skies. There is a voracious beast tied to Polaris, at the end of the big dipper and if he were to break from his chains he would devour the UNIVERSE. So these sisters take shifts looking out for us. They remind us that we won't be thanked for our hard work but that we must continue regardless.

WE ARE THE ZORYA SISTERS

I am one
And two and three
Depending on the stories
You hear of me

The morning star, the evening star
    and the midnight star

We are always watching the skies
Simargl is chained now
Tied tight to Polaris

A death hound
The gryphon
A doomsday bringer
And it is our job to make sure
    he stays put

We take turns
Rising from our sleep

Watching vigilantly
And returning to slumber
    when the
Next takes her post

The world will never know
Both the peril
They were in
And the reason
The sun continues to rise
    each morning

Our home is beautiful
A sanctuary
With slavic gods and
    goddesses adorning our
    walls in paintings and
    tapestries and whispers
Our clothes are finely
    embroidered

Dresses of fine linens
Laces of fine silks
Our hair done up with combs

Quiet is our music
For there is always a gentle
    sleeper in the home
No one visits

The scent of food always
    cooking hangs in the air
Onions, garlic, meat, when we
    can get it
Potatoes
And dark coffee

The air is thick with history
Expectation
Tradition
Ours is a life of duty.

REFLECT

The triad,
the triple goddess, the three fates
A concept that comes up in most cultures in some way
Whether it's the maiden, mother, and crone
The past, present, and future
Truth, Beauty, and Love
Humans are drawn to the three
And each of us has all of them inside us
Reflect on how these concepts are alive in your life
Reflect on the nuances that ripple throughout this
    book and throughout your story
What do you do in your life that no one will ever
    know about?
Reflect on the tragedies that have been avoided
    because of your magic
Your intuitions, your foresight. Thank you.

ACT

Each action you take
Each word you speak and
Each piece of magic you weave
Know that this world is not the same without you
Walk every step with intention
Knowing your steps will ripple out and affect the
    lives around you
You are never alone. You have an army at your side.

MEDITATE

Close your eyes
Breathe in. Acknowledge the magic you have created
Breathe out and know that your breath will carry on
Your breath will become part of the human story
As our ancestors breath is part of our story
Breathe deep
Your home is your heart
Your heart is a river
The breadcrumbs are there for you
To find your way back
Your spirit is part of a neverending story
We are with you.

About Jessica Theroux

Jessica Theroux is an artist and educator renowned for intertwining her personal journey with her artistic pursuits, including embroidery, historical research, and a deep spiritual connection to goddess figures. Through her mastery of needlework, lineart drawings, and poetic expression, she delves into the mystical realms of the feminine divine, shining a light on the power that resides within every cherished and often-overlooked creature on our planet. In a recent TedX talk, she explored the significance of love in our collective journey of (re)creating the world. Jessica lives in Calgary, Alberta, Canada.